When waiting becomes hating

Poetry and lyrics by Adrian Guldahl

When waiting becomes hating

All illustrations © 2024 by Adrian Guldahl
Publisher: BoD – Books on Demand, Oslo, Norge
Print: BoD – Books on Demand, Norderstedt, Tyskland
ISBN: 9788284510972

"People know you
For what you've done
Not for what
You plan to do"

Table of contents

82 - Born cold

83 - Never again

84 - Disunity

85 - Walk the abyss

86 - Warts and all

87 - Wolf

88 - Betrayer

89 - Bedbound

90 - The art of losing a friend

91 - Love

92 - Sorrowjoy

93 - Naysayer

94 - Redflag

95 - Enemy

96 - Night after night

97 - Dream

98 - Freckled

99 - Cain

100 - Sitting in a church

101 - Cherry picking

123 - Nemesis

124 - Gorgon

125 - Ghost of a twisted angel

126 - Banshee

127 - Demonhole

128 - Within

139 - Names

130 - Resurrected

131 - Keep your eyes closed

132 - My war

133 - Malvy

134 - Deliver me

These poems and lyrics have been made over a long period of time. I have decided to release them in this poetry book in order to have some sort of closure.

Castle of rhythm

One look and I was numb
She lived in a castle of rhythm
When I plugged her in
And run my fingers down her strings
Tuned just right. She was a weapon.

There was no escape
As I got cursed by her body shape
She just couldn't be stopped
Peasants or kings
You can't escape her when she sings.

A new product

Welcome to secrets untold!
I was born into this world with a blindfold
Yet it didn't take long
Before I realized my soul was already sold.

Why do we accept that people turn us into machines?
This is why I decided to believe in dreams.

I refuse to be a product
But that's what I am
I am no better, no worse
But I dwell on this curse.

A curse that makes me doubt everything you say
If you wear a suit
I'm not proud of being human
I'm proud of our potential
I'm proud of what we create with our heart
I'm proud of art.

Satisfy my thirst

I recorded an image on film
A blind evil paranormal chess player
I praise appearance and style
As it satisfies my thirst for visual celebration.

Proud of spelling mistakes

I have not written the word In the same way as you
I have stretched the word and made it unique.

I have made a difference
I have not taken the same path as you.

But you do not liike my path and you judge me to fast
Because flaws makes uniqueness
And where you see wrong, I see potential.

Come cowards again

You only live once, Don't forget!
And I'm stuck here with you
Someone without an artistic point of view
I'm stuck with you.

Your lack of dedication makes me doubt myself
There's so much more to music than just sound
Misplaced admiration and wasted education
Doesn't matter what I say, time has already ticked away.

You only live once, Don't forget!
And you're stuck here with me
Someone full of ideas
You're stuck here with me.

And I will not be defeated
By your good damn uncompleted
Dreams and your pain
So come cowards again.

Frustration

I have been dreaming for far too long
Where do I belong?
I must put my visions to the screen
No more, only a dream.

Alone!

The only thing that seems real:
Can you hear my inner self scream out in frustration?

I am truly an emotional wreck
Who is about to crack
Lock me up before I do something crazy
Because I can not control myself anymore
I will give in
To this cruelty within
It doesn't matter how hard I hold on

I give in

A name

A name can keep you from reaching your goals
A name can make you grossly undermine the person.
Changing a name can open a world of artistic opportunities
Or just make you feel better about yourself.

Useless

You are useless to me now
I can't weave you into my life anymore
I won't do the work for you.

I thought I was guiding you
Turns out I was you
Because there are no you.

Just an empty soul
You have nothing to say
And you are just in my way.

Victim

I observe you and write you down
I put you into lyric and rhyme
I make you disappear without a sound
And I make it alright when you're just about to drown.

Laugh at me

I'm original and true
I kept going where others turned
I'm proud to be unschooled
And self taught.

I have my own version
My own stories
And my own way.

I've dreamt

I've dreamt about kill you
I've dreamt about splitting you open with a knife
And carve the word revenge inside you
I've dreamt about slowly eating your flesh piece by piece
I've dreamt about devouring you.

Every time you spoke those words
With no reason other than to hurt
When you told those lies
THOSE FUCKING LIES.

Don't you think for a second
That I have forgotten about you.

Music is my only friend

Time to get my hands dirty again
Everything has been in vain
Years ago I started a band
With a head full of ideas.

I was on the road for revenge
That was my mission
But my plan did not fall into place
I ended up kicking my best friend on bass.

We never talked much after that
A twenty year old friendship got broken just like that.

The band that never play

Rehearsals short and dumb
Never get anything done
Mostly sit and talk
About how much we rock.

Rehearsals short and dumb
Without melody lines or rhythm
Mostly sit and wait
For one day to be great.

Never on time

You have so much to do
And say: it's easy for you.
Your time has no more value than mine
I will move on and I will be fine.

Rock' n roll

Never think, Just get it out
Left with so much doubt
This is what it's all about
Just keep your guitar on.

That's where you belong
What did I do wrong?
Because I can not wake up
From my rock'n roll song.

Every Sound under the sun

She sings her song of joy
For simple ears to enjoy
She screams her pain out in a song
The only place that she truly belongs.

She cries her way through the verse
Her journey, So perverse
Honest and proud
She is not afraid of getting loud.

Compared I'm just a bullet without a gun
And she is every sound under the sun.

Lack of dedication

I've met people like you before
People like you I can buy in a store
If you can't find the time
You take the time.

If you can't walk around
You start to climb
All the places we could have seen
Just think about everything that could have been.

Truth

You couldn't handle the truth
So we lied
Because we didn't want to hurt you
I say fuck that
I don't like that
Come on, wake up and tell me what you think.

When waiting Becomes hating

The more I wait, The more I hate
Everything was great, Now it's too late.

Time has changed me
Waiting has changed me
You have changed me!

NEVERMIND MY
SUICIDE

Silence and peace

Tell me a story
About pride and glory
Tell me a tale
Where the hero doesn't fail.

As time goes by
I keep wondering why
Why did I stay?
To chase these ghosts away.

Let me have a moment
Of silence and peace
Let the worries inside me
Be at fucking ease.

Please just for a moment
Because I want to feel
That a story about love
Is something I don't have to steal.

For my lover

I miss your smile, so smile
Please don't cry, let's forget about the lie
Let's pretend it's all going to be fine
You my lover, you are mine.

And we will run away from it all
Even though we know it is only lyrics to a song
Let's lose our self in this moment
Because tomorrow we will have to face the truth.

So let's pretend it's all going to be fine
You my lover, open the wine
We shall run away from these fools
And rob them of their wealth and jewels.

Wishing well

I'll take you to the movies
I'll take you to a bar
I'll take you to the moon and back
But only leave you scars.

I'll take you to heaven
Before I'll take you to hell
But you must first throw yourself
In the wishing well.

Adam and Evil

Said you cared
Said you'd be there
I want to rip you apart
For every second I wasted with you .

I want you to suffer
For your absence and your ignorance
You're not my first
You're not my last .

I faked my way into your heart
And slowly composed little lies
I can truly say I am even
Good luck Adam and evil.

Hope and soap

It starts with hope but ends with soap
To wash away the pain
Over and over again
Lay down your defenses today and I swear
I will save you
I will help you
I will be there for you.

But when you are defenseless and naked
I will leave you dirty
Lost and hated
I will take away what beauty you had
All the good in you shall be turned bad
And your love story will end so sad
That you will never be able to love again.

The warm winds of seduction

I stare into your soul through your eyes
I strip you from guilt and lies
My smile makes your heart beat fast
And makes nothing matter from your past.

Without shame, Without fear
I slid my fingers through your hair
The words I finally speak shows my intention
And these are the warm winds of my seduction.

Once a week

I wish I could see you much more
All this bullshit in the way What's it all for?
Money, Buss and train
If I can't see you once a week
I swear I'll go insane.

I want to wake up with billions of dollars
So I could spend a few
No I'd spend it all on you
I'd take you away
Far from buss and train
I know that dream will never come true
But it doesn't matter as long as I have you once a week.

Rip out

I go into the land of death
When I take another breath
I know I'll miss you to death
I know it's hard to confess.

But you blessed me with your fingers crossed
You took my soul when I was lost
So I took the pills yesterday, just to feel numb
Yeah I took the pills yesterday
And now look what I've become.

I do anything to have you now
And I do anything to defeat you
I do anything to make you feel like
You are lost.

I feel forced to write down what I feel
But there is nothing left to reveal
Only hatred
Hatred and pain.

I will rip out all my piercings
I will make a new tattoo
But now I'm sending all of my hate
And anger into you.

I will cut off all my fingers
And mail them to you
But now I'm sending all of my hate
And anger into you.

I go into the land of death
When I take my final breath
I wasted so much time on you
So many hours and if you knew.

You wouldn't break a heart like this
And build me up to be so pissed
I don't exist, I don't exist, I don't, I DON'T!
Because I loved you and I always will.

Relationshit

Hey I must say
That I feel trapped
Like I can't move
Like I'm strapped.

To a chair
It's unfair
When you say
I don't care.

I really love you
I really do
But I can't breathe
So what should I do?

Body piercing

Putting the needle into the skin is pain
But it is worth it because of the great pleasure
When the needle pierces through
It's like a great release, like an orgasm.

A feeling of sensual intimacy and overwhelming love
It's like the perfect song
That makes you unable to resist the urge of singing along.

It's my sickness
My addiction
And my salvation.

Champaign
For the pleasure of pain.

The rambling crazy man

I will be the rambling crazy man
With a beer bottle in my hand
I will walk the street, bare feet
And never eat anything but shit.

I will give up all my dreams
To sit on a corner begging for money
For drugs and alcohol.

I will steal at the mal
Being ignored by all
And always feel small.

And you will always be that guy
That keeps asking me why
I have a beer bottle in my hand
And why I am the rambling crazy man.

Classroom of dead people

Mother forced me to go to school today
I said please don't because they hate me in every way
I entered the classroom
I came in late.

I could feel the anger and the overwhelming hate
All the people there started talking behind my back
And the devil of a teacher got ready for her attack
What are seven times eight?
She asked with a voice full of hate.

She said the answer was fifty six
I thought to myself am so sick of this
A guy sitting behind me whispered:
Stupid freckled fuck.

The girl next to me said: No he's not but yes he sucks
The rest of the day all I could do was sit and smile
Because that day I killed them all in my mind
And It was just me and a classroom full of dead people.

FriEND

Tell me where's my friend?
Who will defend me to the end?
We used to be like brothers
You took my worries of my shoulders
Who has replaced me?
Has she replaced me so easily?

Mind

I'm so glad for you
I'm so glad that you will never see what's on my mind
You will never have to see the horrible images
I create in my head.

Because in my head
Devils are being eaten for joy
Beautiful angels are being corrupted
And assigned to destroy.

My mind is a product of what you created
A disease unstoppable and incurable.

Drunk

My body is lying on the bathroom floor
I have been puking for days
And I can't take anymore
I have been drinking my sorrows away.

I can't tell you what happened
because I haven't been sober for days
Maybe she took my pride away
Maybe because I have lost so many friends these days.

Maybe it was because my band broke up
Maybe it was… Oh wait...; Sorry, I had to throw up!
I forgot what I was saying but it doesn't matter anymore
Because I'm on my way to the liquor store.

Help

Help me
And help me again

I don't confess
Before in quicksand

Help me
And help yourself

But nobody understand
Except the rope In my hand.

Nevermind my suicide

This is the beginning of the end
You are my only friend
What am I doing here?
Please take it all away.

I hate my self for what I do
Not for what I am
So please tell me what to do
You know I do it for you.

I always said something wrong
Never laughed, Never smiled
She told me:
keep your smile and laugh all day.

I don't know why I walk around,
following you
Maybe this will go to hell
And I can't take it anymore.

Now death is here for my soul
So you can begin this war
Because I'm tired but I will remain
So you can be the first to say:

Now you're dead but not forgotten
I dig you up and fuck you rotten
I want to die so don't cry
But never mind my suicide.

Because everybody is going to die
My final word will be goodbye
For every month, for every week
And because all we do is live.

I'm burning away
And I'm better off dead.

Paranoia

Feeling kind of paranoid
Watching my own funeral
Someone is watching me
And I just want to feel free.

But I'm the one that can't be free
Because I'm the one who's left to see
That someone is controlling me
Anyway just leave me be.

I feel the darkness follow me
It's like a movie on TV
Where I'm good and you are bad
You haunt me every night.

Got everything you said
All about F.U.C.K
Must get these voices out of my head
Before I fade away.

You want me to fall
So you can bring me down
You're the one who hope
That I'm paranoid.

You want me to fall
So you can bring me down
Yeah you want me to fall
So you can call me paranoia.

I ask myself: where should I go?
You make me feel so alone
And I don't know what I have done
Just give me something to relax on.

Because this paranoia is driving me insane
I can see you everywhere
And I can breathe but not escape
So please just go away.

Respite

I've lost my faith in love
So death here I come
Was this my faith?
A fucked up person you can hate.

I am ready and set
How deadish can I get?
Because today I realize
You're not a noble price.

Death awaits me now
I'm lost on the road somehow
And I feel crushed and numb
In your knowledge I am dumb.

So don't you walk away
Because I got things to say
And today I realize
You're not a fucking noble price.

I am so forsaken
My life has been taken
So fuck it all
My respite will come.

Drowning in sorrows

The pain shows you're alive
I'm behind enemy lines
This life is painted gray
And I'm drifting away.

You don't know what you have
Before you have lost it
In this land without sun
I reload my gun.

I think about you everyday
Think so much I could kill myself
Got a piece of paper you touched
Keep it safe and kiss it a lot.

You don't know what you have
Before you have lost it
In this land without sun
I reload my gun.

I am drowning in sorrows
And you are the key to salvation.

When I see you I will lose my wounds
I only live for you
Your eyes glitters as a star
I wouldn't tell you if it was a lie.

I confess it all to the rain
Then locked it all away
They just want their cash
So they can wipe their own ass.

You don't know what you have
Before you have lost it
In this land without sun
I reload my gun.

Care at all

Life was not so great
Before you went away
I pictured you this way
Before you went away.

It's just another day
With sorrow and pain
It's just another day
I think I slipped away.

What is wrong with me?
Am I really to blind to see?
I'm feeling like a fool
Because I was just your tool.

I should have known better
Than giving all of me away
But you know what they say
Everything will end someday.

So if I fall into hell
Would you drag me up again?
And if I fade, way too fast
Would you make sure it didn't last?

Out of light and into dark
From good to bad, from happy to sad
Would you care? Care at all
If you find me when I fall.

Another coin in your wallet

I can't go back to another road
So I go into the unknown
I've walked this road for so long
But still have so much more to come.

If I were the picture would you be the frame?
If you were the picture would you feel the same?
Because you're my roof against all rain
But still the darkness will remain.

I've walked so long and I need a rest
I need a break to find myself
It looks like the time's been standing still
And it was all against my will.

Outside the shadows covers me
So you won't see me bleed
Now I'm standing in the rain
But still the shadows will remain.

I wish we could be, I wish you could see
I wish you had feelings just for me
And it's growing stronger everyday
And I can't turn and run away
Am I just another coin in your wallet?

Hidden Love

She won't look me in the eye
She would rather die
But won't leave her for a queen
Am I lost inside a dream?

She's got eyes just like the stars
And her mouth speak no lies
She got hair just like the wind
And her lips would surly sin.

These kingdoms exist for only few
Maybe just for me and you
These kingdoms exist for only few
Maybe just for you.

She's the one and only one
Letting go would be so dumb
She's so pretty when she dance
Hope we die holding hands.

She won't look me in the eye
She would rather die
She was more than just a friend
But now I'll surely write the end.

First wave

Behind closed doors,
Something new is taking form
Something new, something bad
From sweet child to dirty rat.

Now look into my eyes
You'll see this flame that burns in my mind
Now tell me why
You hate my stuff all the time.

But I don't care what you say
Because this flame that burns will never burn away
So tell me why, why I am the empty soul
But I will never go.

I wish I was a fish
Living in the sea
Yeah I wish I was a fish
Looking for the meat.

Because here I do not bleed
Here all seem to heal
But maybe I don't see
That it's something in the deep.

So breath it in, spit it out
Break a leg and tell me why
You're going down
In my first wave.

Drink tears

I've felt lonely, I've felt blue
I never felt these things with you.
It's christmas morning when am writing this
Thinking there's a person I miss.

Love your skin and what's within
Wonder what tomorrow might bring
Bored of waiting, I feel blue
Might have something to do with you.

And I drink your tears away

I feel happy, I feel good
I feel things I thought I never would
The wait is over and I don't feel blue
Only six more days until I see you.

I've been broken, I've been lost
So pick me up, no matter the cost
Be my light, stay up all night
You'll be fine and shine all bright.

And I drink your tears away

New years eve and I'm writing this
The bloody bitch broke my heart with a kiss
It took me six hours to get home
And now I suffer alone.

The pleasure of pain

All these memories, puts me down to my dirty knees
I can't believe but it's so real, all this anger that I feel
You can't hurt me anymore, you are just a dirty whore
I'm so wasted, I'm so drunk and I'm an idiot playing punk.

Now it's time to let it go, now it's time to let you know
I can not survive all this, everyone just makes me pissed
All these lies this bitch said has made me feel dead
So put me in a grave, I'd rather die than be a slave.

What more can I do? I know I did it all for you
This is what I came to say, now it's time for you to pay
Life's a bitch, so are you and now I've said it all for you
You think it's over but it's not, that's because it never stops.

Pain goes on and so do you
Even though you don't want to
Yeah I'll give you pleasure
The pleasure of pain.

Fuck it all

I can't take this life no more
I hate this shit, I hate it all
I stand up but then I fall
So I scream fuck it all.

So many times I wish I was dead
So many times I wish I said:
You were never there for me
You blinded me so I couldn't see.

I tried to crawl back to the free
But no one was there for me
I was the snowball you threw into hell
And all my life I wanted to tell.

Time and time I tried to say
Give me a reason, why should I stay?
But you just let me fade away
When I thought I was here to stay.

And now the time has come for me
This is the last words you'll hear from me
I don't care what you say
I will get my revenge anyway.

This is the last time that I crawl
So now bitch I just fuck it all
I leave this world, no more pain
I leave this world and end the game.

Swirl

Clouds lose shape
Blind lost landscape
Always bedtime
Perfect for crime
Where souls swirl
A grey world.

Self Abused

My tragedy

I put needles into my arm
Again I do myself some harm
Nobody can make me stop
I will do this until I drop.

I pretended I was someone else
The drug was my true romance
I was hiding from the truth
And it destroyed my youth.

I don't need your blasphemy
As I have survived my tragedy
It was a needle made out of the devil's eyes
And the devil sang me lullabies.

I cheated death one too many times
Hurting myself is one of my biggest crimes
But I didn't die at age twenty three
Because I found it in my heart to forgive myself.

Friendly enemy

Suicide is not a crime
Paulina said I lost my mind
This friendship ain't so tied
So buy me a homicide.

Drunk in Cyprus made me smile
Victoria made me happy for a while
But now I'm a bringer of sorrow
Am I Norman Bates tomorrow?

Paulina please on my knees
Paulina please, please, please
Paulina please stand in line
Suicide is not a crime.

I don't believe what I hear and se
Paulina said I was a wannabe
Hey don't you ever judge me
She never comes to visit me.

She told me to believe
And sing: let it be
Does she want me to be?
A fucking friendly enemy.

Wanting death

No matter how much I want it
Not matter how much I try
Who's going to be here
To wipe my tears dry?

I'm pushed from every side
I got to keep this deep inside
It dropped tears from eye
The day we said goodbye.

No matter what I do
Other thoughts are replaced by you
Because the good old times are gone
Now I'm just living on.

Waiting for a call
or someone at the door
But there's no one there at all
Because the good old times are gone.

All my friends are gone
There names spinning in my head
I remember you Liz, I remember you Chris
And all the others on the list.

Why does everyone I don't want to know live close to me?
And everyone I want to know lives far from me.
This was the kingdom that existed for few
For a while it was for me and for a while it was for you.

All my friendships goes down like titanic
And now I'm in panic
Because what if I never see you again
What if we never ever meet again?

So I want death
I don't want another breath
Yes I want death;
Good memories ain't always the best.

Art is my religion!

The girl

She will always be a part of my world
Because I will never forget this girl
I sat next to her for so many years
And I just couldn't take my eyes off her.

I would just sit and stare
Looking all dumb and feeling so numb
Because I was stunned by her smile
She had a troubled mind.

Her voice was a musical masterpiece to my ears
Her spoken words was a spiritual poetry reading
And her beauty, an artwork of a thousand painters.

A smile full of lies

I'm cold, my lips are blue
It was different with you
My body is drifting in space
I remember the rain on my face.

How much worse can it get
Have you buried me yet?
I'm naked no disguise
Too many sweet goodbyes.

I embrace the ending
When nothing's changing
All these scars in my skin
Makes me feel good within.

But even as it please me
This won't complete me
Show me a beautiful sunrise
And I'll show you a smile full of lies.

Dualism

In order to have good
You must have bad.

Join me in the body bag

I want to frame you with love
Make you see the end and rebuild you again
Our sins will never die In spite of our beautiful lies
Because we are consumed by our lust.

When all our dreams turns to dust
You can't cut down what always grow
Refused, abused
Confused love.

I found a place for two
A space for me and you
Let's pierce our souls together
Come join me in the body bag.

Well dressed for emptiness

No art, no heart
Strange views, strange clues
Grow up, drink up
No sleep, only weep.

Destroyed
Unemployed
Corruption
Eruption.

You are only a friend for the title.

My scrambled words

Bones
Suffering
Disorder
Rage

Rip the flesh from the bone
And watch them scream before they mourn

Empty emotion
Heart all frozen
Words spoken
Promises broken

Hidden
Forbidden
Paint a picture
Sing a song
Write some words
But don't wait long

As you are
Speaking down
To me
I shall
Speak to you!

p E R f E C T I O N!

Copy

What mind
Out of line
Not alive
No time.

Your creation
Your education
Dysfunction
Malfunction.

Numbers

Wake up and sleepwalk to work
Seconds away from going berserk

Fuck your perfection
Your biggest erection

You seem dumber
When it's all about a number

Art and Nature

Bible of depression and science of obsession
My God is not forced upon me
Those who believe in my God
Is often looked upon with great pity
I swear no oath, I believe a little in both.

Brainwashed world of shame

Brainwashed
Empty and lost
Break free from the curse
Whatever the cost.

Don't let people control you
You have more potential than being a slave
Rise above it and make a name
Fight their game or drown in shame.

Be lame, adore fame
And always remain the same.

Cry with the whole face

Who cares about some falling tears
Some broken hearts, some wasted years
So sad and so bad
You cry until you die.

Hiding away behind a mask
Forgetting about the task
And while the world infiltrates your space
All you can do is cry with the whole face.

Run the risk

I run the risk when I say these words
I love the truth so fuck what you've heard
Nobody wants you so on anger you feed
Driven by hatred and all around greed.

I hate people and people hate me too
I hate people, I hate you.

Respect

Don't judge anyone
That feels art in their heart
Be a good person
Respect the individual.

Don't point the gun
Without leaving room for fun
Be honest
And be proud of what you've become.

Angel of Prostitution

See me rise from the ruin
Revenge for what you've been doing
Smiling at your execution
The angel of prostitution.

Cute little dead girl

Drag the dead kitty
Along the floor
All the way
To the bathroom door.

Died so young
And always looking for fun
But always ends up
Killing some.

Princess

Into the sea
The frog she sat free
The water reflect
Her, far from perfect.

The water so cold
Her body and soul
And the flowers will rot
Because he forgot.

Heaven too beautiful

Broken down, do you feel blue?
Are demons surrounding you?
Behind every wall
There's a war going on.

No angels in between
The demons in me scream
It all seems like a dream
Is heaven too beautiful for me?

Beneath the surface of my thoughts, I am
Engaged with evil, I can not escape the
Devil in me. The devil
Left me here as a madman.
Alive enough to ramble crazy
More can not be said.

Echo

Echo in the wind
Of childish empty sin
Laughter and joy
For the evil deeds we enjoy.

Like A whisper in the wind
Her voice so gently sings
Help me lord
For death is near.

Swarm

Across a sea of tears
A hundred thousand years
Forget the person you kissed
And stay with me in the mist.

Look at my demons
As they swarm around the room
As the ghost from my past
Arise from the tomb.

Here to punish me
For my early sins
Yes this is where
My damnation begins.

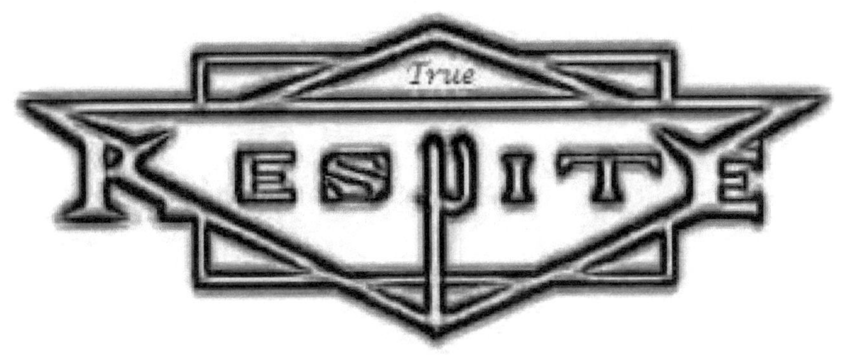

True
RESPITE

Purpose and intention

Let's move forward without looking back
Let's focus on the issue and get back on track
Strength and power
To overcome the hour.

Where a politician fails
An artist prevails
Together we will stand
And make you understand.

WARNING!

Animals acting like animals.

Meaningless

I suffer through
A mental struggle
When I write
I get too deep.

I am building up a wall
I won't let anyone in anymore
I am sealing up the door
I don't want anything at all.

I'll confess
Am a mess
It's all meaningless.

?? ?? ?????? ?? ???????
?? ?? ?? ?? ?? ??
??????? ?????? ?? ???????
?? ?? ?? ?? ??
?? ?? ?????? ?????? ??

Ashtray

A devil from the sky
An angel living a lie
To protect and serve
As shadows burn.

History has turned us drifting apart
We played from the heart
Only to forget where we started
As we pulled two headed girlfriends apart.

The truth is we were glue
And no one will know respite like we do.

Photo album

I've gone through a couple of photo albums
And crossed out every person I don't like
Their heads have been decapitated
Their eyes are cut out with scissors.

Some has gotten arrows through their heads
Some are just looking ghoulish and dead
Others are crying or screaming in pain
It looks funny but insane.

One person I've left alone
Because she was the only one
I've painted a heart around her head
But when I am done, I bet even she will be dead.

"I used a lot of red colors that day"

Valentines Day

Screw it, Let's do it
I knew it, you blew it
You couldn't handle the truth
It's Valentine's Day.

Honest and proud
Sometimes silent
Sometimes loud
Screw it, Let's do it.

Sister

You should be able to smile much more
Because no other creature deserves it more.

I'm a pest and a plague
That drags you with me
Anywhere and everywhere
The lost and the broken.

Let's laugh again.

Descendant

Stop all this
We came here in a Viking Ship
Honored among the gods
Berserkers.

Valhalla awaits me
Odin awaits me
The runes has been carved
And my sword starved.

Threaten me with hell
You forget that I know well
The vikings are my forefathers
I'm a descendant.

Anything else

Just another sad song to sing
Isn't there anything else I can bring?
I survived the sea
It's ok, there is nothing else I need to be.

I don't need revenge anymore
Anything else? I have settled the score
I will save a princess along the way
Seriously, I'm ok and there's nothing else left to say.

DreadMist

Born Cold

I was born in the north
In cold winds and snow
Where trees are endless
In shades and shadow.

On frozen lakes we play
Behind mountains of old
A winter clad landscape
In mist and fog.

Lost in woods we found a way
To look ahead for better days
And you can't hurt me at all
because I was born cold.

Comfort in old fairy tales
Old sagas and tales of battle
The rain brings me sadness
Before we're swallowed by the sun.

In stones we carve our past
In frost we survive
A Fisherman's goldmine
And a farmer's struggle.

This is the place I want to grow old
A place where you can remove the blindfold
The shackles and chain
The only place to keep me sane.

Never again

You took your time, stepped out of line
Never asked if I was fine
Your words are hollow, empty and shallow
You are just a fool.

I won't be used, battered and bruised
You must be confused
Cuz in the end you were not a friend
Just someone who pretend.

You can cause me pain, keep me in chain
Mess with my brain, then call me insane
Try to drown me in rain, then in champagne
Now and then but never again.

I'm someone new, I'm judged by you
But I know what is true
I've changed a lot, I untie the knot
And release myself from it all.

You're such a bore, right to you're core
Never answer when I call
Drop to the floor, run out that door
You're not welcome anymore.

Disunity

There was always a lie in your smile
And a scorpion between those thighs
As you make your bed, you must lie in it
And don't you forget about it.

You won't get no empathy
Or love from me.

I bought a box of twenty five
I Was up all night to put things right
I heal my scars as I finish cigars
And I smoked about half, with a broken heart.

There's lies in your beauty
So show me the real you
Show me you.

Walk the abyss

At night I come alive
Can you tell me why?
In a candle lit room
I find comfort in the gloom.

The sorrow and the hurt
I have buried in the dirt
Cloaked in shadow
My imagination run's wild.

Please just let the sun go down
Only darkness knows me now.

Help me solve this riddle
And don't you let me dwindle
In silence and a gentle breeze
I'm more alive when you're asleep.

Only on a night like this
Will I walk in the abyss
It's time that you wake up
And It's time you walk with me.

Warts and all

Here I am, warts and all
Cigars and alcohol
I don't want to look back
Or de-rail from the track.

Cast this self doubt aside
Along with self-esteem and pride
Please don't let me get me
I'm hyped on too much coffee
It's hard to concentrate
Stand still or see straight.

Give me something for my hangover
It ain't easy when you're always starting over
Give me a pill to face the fear
Fuck it, ill just have another beer.

What do you have against shame
I'll take whatever you got for the pain
I don't know maybe i'm going insane
Let's celebrate with some champagne.

Wolf

A wolf doesn't lose sleep
Over the opinions of sheep
Stay your ground
Or turn and flee.

You can lead
Or you can follow me
Fight to be free
Or bend the knee.

This is the choice you will have to make.
Wolf or sheep!

Come speak your mind
Or get back in line
Now walk the walk
Or talk the talk.

Speak try me
Or why me
Learn to be brave
Or learn to behave.

Make yourself a sheep
And the wolves will eat you.

Betrayer

This I unfold, all my secrets untold
I cannot belong, don't you tell me am wrong
I have no solution, I'm lost in confusion
For all my delusions, that's my conclusion.

I have nothing for you
And nothing is what you will get.

Paranoia slips in
And I want to give in
Tomorrow will be a brighter day
But that day is not today.

I thought you were my savior
But you were my betrayer.

Bedbound

Feels like I'm living on borrowed time
Modern medicine has kept me alive
I'm chained to a bed again
It's not a lie, I would have died.

Fill my lounges with air,
Let me be high on anesthetics again
Let me be delirious and apathetic,
Cuz I don't wanna be bed bound no more.

All I see are nurses in white
Asking questions without answers
I'm hitting a new low
Walls are white, way too bright.

I am so delirious,
Why are you so serious
Everything's hilarious
And I am so delirious.

My identity is on the line
I'm getting close to losing my mind
The pain is unbearable
Kill it now, kill it now.

Get me out of this place, no more surgery ok?
With these scars, in this way, I'm just a lab rat today.

The art of losing a friend

I don't even know where to begin
No matter what I do I just can't win
These memories are rotten
They should all be forgotten.

I won't wait for tomorrow
Just to greet my old sorrow
I will cover the world with my misery
And all I will achieve is a sinister me.

This whole thing is long overdue
This time I don't walk around
but cut my way through.

There is an end in friend
And good in goodbye
Everything comes to an end
The art of losing a friend.

I am just a shadow of a man
I know you'll never understand
I don't make time for people
who don't make time for me.

I will change my tone and walk alone
Quell this feeling, and stop the bleeding
I never wanted it to end this way
But in the end someone's gotta pay.

Love

Wrap yourself around me like a snake
Then slider right back into the lake
Cause I can feel the venom on your tongue
And I don't like what I've become.

I can see you force yourself to smile
Just to make me happy for awhile
I don't feel great, can you relate?
Now all my love has turned to hate.

Whatever this is
It ain't love.

Sorrowjoy

You always ask me
Why don't you write something happy
Something to make me smile
Just for a while.

Because you are not this sad
And you are not this bad
So put some flowers in
Put more colors in.

But when you're happy, I cannot relate to you
When you're happy, It always feels so fake to me
When you're happy, I cannot relate to you
When you're happy, that is not how I truly feel.

I won't ask of you
To lie about what you go through
Make up more lies
And never ask why.

Because you are not this happy
And you are not this good
So put some thorns in
Put some darkness in.

Naysayer

The hardest walk you take
Is the walk you take alone
I tune out when you speak
Destroyer of dreams.

I rather suffer alone
Then sit on your paper throne
I live to prove you wrong
Alone but never felt this strong.

I won't shed a tear
Or give in to fear
You without vision
Killer of ambition.

Learn to live with failure
Than change your behavior
You the dreamslayer
You the naysayer.

Impossible is only for you
I learn to break through
Why is there blood?
Blood on your hands.

Redflag

She's in love with these 4 letters
more than she loves me
I don't recognize myself
My body don't agree with me.

I try my best but im still a mess
And now I feel depressed
And it's wrong of me to blame you
But I do.

Im still young enough to be dumb enough
To say that I love you
And am the emperor and the sea
And I will show you what darkness lies in me.

My voice is not deep enough
And my dick is not big enough
Complain is her middle name
A redflag playing a game.

Enemy

If I knew then what I know now
I wouldn't wait and give fuel to my hate
I'm done with the jokes and the false hope
Everybody shut up.

You should fear me
I am not as innocent
As you make me out to be
You awoke something dark in me.

From january to december
I will never surrender
no excuses for me
You can doubt me and belittle me.

Night after night

This is a note to a bully
The one that I hate fully
I remember everything
And I can't forget anything.

In my dreams where I do crimes
I have killed you a thousand times
I have no remorse and no regret
I just can't forget.

I don't believe in forgiveness
And if you do, you've never walked in my shoes
I don't believe in forgiveness
You die night after night.

It's your time to be the victim
I'll be the poison in your system
You will forever fuel my fire
Right up until the day I expire.

You may have changed your ways
But I will judge you until the end of days
I imagine you six feet under ground
How you would look the minute that you drown.

Dream

Get out of my way
I got things to say
I got bills to pay
I got bricks to lay.

Let me be selfish and alone
I can't be broken, I just move on
If I can't walk around
I start to climb.

I dream big
but graves I dig.

I don't have boundaries
I don't see stop signs
you can't keep me down
Dressed to kill.

My dream was dust, broken by trust
My feelings was hurt but not enough
No valley to deep, no mountain too tall
I will conquer it all.

Freckled

Don't you tell me to turn the other cheek
Don't you tell me that I am weak
Cause I will murder you in your sleep
And I will enjoy it when you scream.

All my freckles are bullets meant for you
No mercy from me, no matter what you do
I have a killed a part of me to stay alive
I'm a loner and I'm different now.

You dont know all the demons I've wrestled
Freckled

This feeling of being left in the gutter again
I can not shake your hand
I wish I had some love for you
I wish I knew what to do.

I wish I could make it alright
But it ain't right when you're freckled.

Cain

You rejected my offerings
You favor my brother
I was forced to walk the land
You could never understand.

I am rain
I am pain
I am Cain

You banished me from the soil
I am the age of darkness
The first murderer
I am sinful.

Sitting in a church

Sitting in a church
Looking at a cross
Listening to a priest say
It is comfort for your loss.

But from carlin i've learned
To question everything
And from hitchens that religion
poisons everything.

Science doesn't know everything
But religion doesn't know anything
Let's not judge people on how they look
And never trust anyone with just one book.

Cherry picking

Better learn to cherry pick
Read the good stuff, avoid the sick
Love the thing that makes you smile
The bandage makes it better for a while.

Ignore the verse that makes it worse
It's easy when your the center of the universe
From you twisted views
You cite the bible and pick and choose.

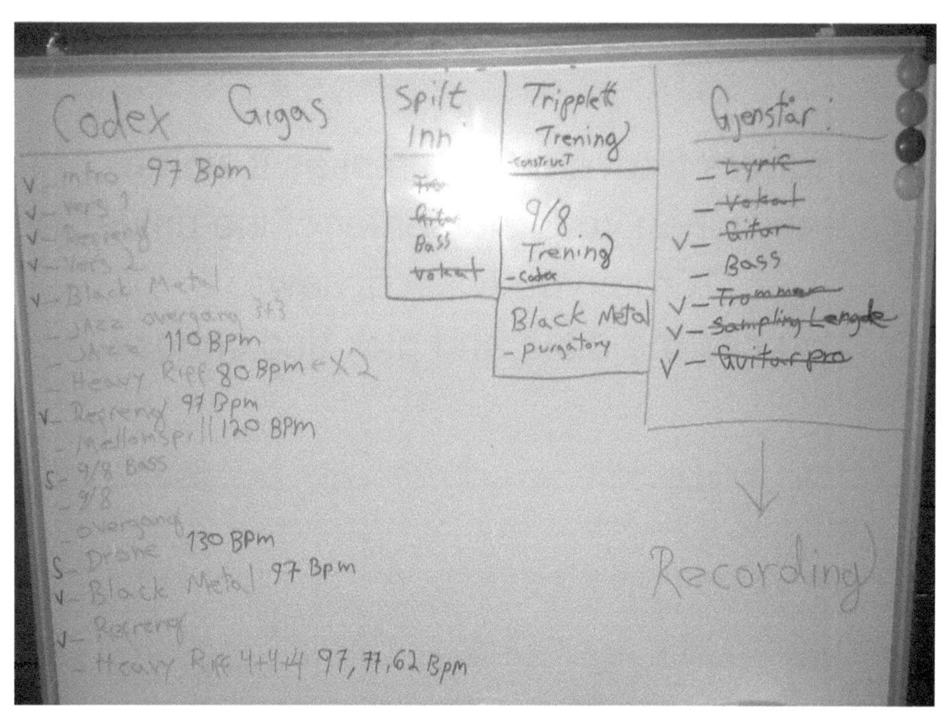

Codex Gigas

v - intro   97 Bpm
v - Vers 1
v - Refreng
v - Vers 2
v - Black Metal
  - Jazz overgang 3+3
  - Jazz   110 Bpm
  - Heavy Riff 80 Bpm - X2
v - Refreng 97 Bpm
  - Mellomspill 120 BPM
S - 9/8 Bass
  - 9/8
  - overgang
S - Drone   130 BPm
v - Black Metal 97 Bpm
v - Refreng
  - Heavy Riff 4+4+4 97, 77, 62 Bpm

Spilt Inn
Fri
Gitar
Bass
Vokal

Tripplet Trening
- construct

9/8 Trening
- Codex

Black Metal
- purgatory

Gjenstår:
- Lyric
- Vokal
v - Gitar
  - Bass
v - Trommer
v - Sampling Lengde
v - Guitar pro

Recording

Atheist

Your god is not great
No evidence for faith
Challenge your belief
And you will feel relief.

If faith is a choice
Than it can be lost
Faith is not the answer
Religion is a cancer.

A man watching from afar

A man watching from afar
Casting a be-winged shadow
You can follow the inc
But don't get lost in the words
Before the enlightenment
Before science
In Deadly disease and superstition
Another book created to control.

In life there's beauty, through pain and love we stumble
We have every reason to live
Death is certain, replacing both the siren-song
Of paradise and dread of hell.

Fundamentalist
There is nothing more
But I want nothing more.

Fundamentalist
Common sense is a flower
That doesn't grow in your garden.

Human beings, reap the fruits of madness
And consider them holy
But we're the mammals, dependent on the web of nature
With a moral compass in hand.

Codex gigas

Page after page he writes
Until his hand gets numb
Another one sells his soul
As he pleads for his life.

Encapsulate
All earthly knowledge
In one night.

Walled up brick by brick
As punishment for his sins
His hand is guided
And saved by the fallen one.

As your prison of belief takes away all logic
listen to reason and look for the truth
you traded drugs for faith and lost your mind
It's time you get hitch-slapped back around.

Exorcism

We are the ones who dwell within
We bring death, pain and sin
I am the one who dwelt within Cain
By jealousy we drove him insane.

The smell of something burning
The sound of knuckles twisting
And I was with Legion
Demonic possession.

I am the one who dwelt within Nero
The libertine and the anti hero
Forever remember, never surrender
Forever remember, never surrender.

I am Belial, without worth
A fallen angel, brings death to earth
But the devil in flesh I prefer
Don't you know I'm Lucifer?

Falling angel, rising demon

Forgive, O Lord, my little joke on thee,
And I'll forgive the great big one on me
Stories sell but the facts will tell
Of a rising ape and not heaven or hell.

Falling angel, rising demon

Don't raise more devils then you can lay down
A heretic burns in the middle of town
Dont flirt with angels because they all lie
Like Mother Teresa singing lullabies.

Construct of imagination

Beautiful yet so obscene
Both your houses so unclean
If deception is a way to lie
Then may we never look to the sky.

Both are houses in your mind
The stories of them made you blind
In the end they have the same vision
Are you damaged by religion?

Is heaven and hell the same?
Punishment and discipline
Is God's grace smeared with sin?
Is the devil good or just the same?
And in that case who's left to blame?

One man's heaven another's hell
One embrace it, another rebels
The truth to finally be revealed
In the dreaded mist at the battlefield.

As above so below .

Purgatory

Echoes in the wind
Of childish empty sin
A black forest filled with mist
Walk through mud and stone
Through fields of blood and bone
As evil lurks behind you.

Hunted day and night
All in black and white
Rivers filled with lies
As the sky begins to cry.

Days are weeks and weeks are years
Hide your fear and hide your tears
Dreams unkind, left behind
You lose your mind and track of time.

Free your mind
Leave this place behind
Walk into the sun
Walk into the sun

For a glimpse of hope
A glimps of hope
But in the state of grace
Just an empty space.

When days are cold
When days are cold
Revelations rolling of your tongue
These frozen times
These darkened skies
When pieces of heaven is falling down

Words get lost when I speak them
Feelings change when I feel them
All this pain and misery
In the Ruins of Purgatory.

Can you find hope?
In places where all is lost
You better remember your past
Or you're condemned to repeat it again.

You were never destined for heaven
you were never meant to get in
When will you accept your fate
And see that heaven has closed its gate.

Here at the end of all things
You are lost.

History of hate

At forty nine and sixty one
He sold his soul and it begun
Now The angel fall as the demon rise
Darkness,blood,lice,frogs and flies.

The obvious conclusion is evolution
The obvious resolution is retribution
Blind their eyes to religion
And deathen ears when they preach
There rose another war with heaven.

You, who never question why
Who accept these books
These words and these lies
The truth that's told with bad intent
Beats all lies that you can invent.

Like A man made faith with a history of hate
The crusades and the burning of Bruno at the stake.

Paganborn

For all the pagan born
That didn't conform
Never forget
How they used to behave.

Devour the lie
To keep the smile
Avoid the sick
That's the trick.

Poludnica

It's the hottest part of the day
A young woman dressed in white
Roam the field at noon.

She stop you in the field
To ask you questions
Or engage in conversations.

Don't delay to answer
Smile without sadness
Or taste madness.

Evil lurks by the water

Evil lurks by the water
Sirens bring a lamb to the slaughter
He's blinded to the rocks all around him
He's frozen, paralyzed and he can't swim.

The sorrowful death angel abused
The one she set out to seduce
His body and soul the waves devoured
Death came swift in his final hour.

The ghost of unburied legends
An island full of evil intentions
His eyes are for her alone
The reef will be his gravestone.

From the party to the funeral

From the party to the funeral
I've been through it all.

Lean on you

I lean on you
Sorry but it's true
It shouldn't be me
It should be you
But i'm the one
Who lean on you.

Prison of belief

As your prison of belief
Brings you to your knees
You read another page
From your sad and lonely cage.

Blasphemy

Burn me, burn me
I'm a witch
Make a martyr
Out of this bitch.

I criticize your disguise
And I will not apologize
I don't forget, i won't forget
A modernized suffragette.

Politician

A politician is a clown
In search of a crown.

Respect your madness

We still dwell within
We've been through thick and thin
I am the one who sit in your church
And listens to priests defy all research.

The witches have been burning
The lessons we've been learning
More history of sadness
It is hard to respect your madness.

Broken

her lips stinks or evil words to come
But she's so pretty, she's so young
I had to do it, couldn't resist that tongue
I should have known what was to come.

I broke myself in order to feel alive
I sit awake without any reasons
The memory is the least of my worries now.

Feed us

I know u dont need us
But please just feed us
I do no harm
I'm no treat to you.

Please don't take my space
Don't spit in my face.

I know u dont need us
But please just feed us
Please don't leave us
One day you will need us.

Screaming in the mirror

I have been screaming in the mirror
I have walked with the dead
I im a dead poet and im fucked up in the head
The voice inside is leaking out
Somebody shut the door and then turn off the light.

Open your eyes and don't run for your life
Don't keep it inside, let's put up a fight
Now your having this feeling
That you're forced into believing.

I feel like i'm gonna explode inside
And I feel like this all the time
This is exorcism for brainwashing
Keep thy religion to thyself.

I have been looking at the sealing
And I've been having this feeling
That somethings gone wrong
Terribly wrong.

I have done all the things in your bloody book
I was surprised how little time it took
Your lips stinks of evil words to come
But I'll let you be wrong and i'll let you be dumb
Because spiritual guidance means music to me
And no priest can argue with me.

Nemesis

I am the daughter of justice
I am the Nemesis
Keep your blind faith in me
And Vengeance will set you free.

The divine spirit of the Nemesis
Goddess of retribution
I have the righteous anger
And I am feared and revered.

I punish your evil deeds
Excessive pride and good fortune
Undeserved happiness
And the absence of moderation.

Evil shouldn't look this good
Evil shouldn't look this goddamn good.

Gorgon

Blood from the right
Brings the dead back to life
Blood from the left
Takes your life.

Her wings are of gold
Eyes turn you to stone.

Skin of a serpent
Snakes for hair
It is the gorgon
That you should fear.

Brazen claws
Tusks of boars
Three vicious sisters
Arise from the shore.

Ghost of a Twisted Angel

I appear as mist and I come as fog
I don't need to pray and I don't need a hug
I never ever swallow pain
It keeps me from going insane.

I whisper things into your ear
The room goes cold, you stink of fear
Check your pulse and breath real slow
There's things about me that you don't know.

My past is blurry only some remain
My life was boring and death insane
Your life I'll take for my own
As your name is now carved in stone.

Banshee

Someone is about to die
A banshee wails nearby
At night in the woods
You can hear her mourning call.

Washing the blood stained clothes
Of those who are about to die.
The hag of the mist
The Banshee.

She appear before the death
And warn the family
Someone is about to die
A banshee wails nearby.

Demonhole

Covered in codes
Symbols and stones
Cross the border
For the new world order.

Who's to say Who's right or wrong
Chaos will reign Where demons belong.

The few over the many

Built on false truth
To misguide the youth
Undermine To control
Truth unfold
A hell hole
No soul
Demonhole.

Within

Right under the surface of the skin
Coming out from within
Incarnation of evil inside
Out from the mist of my mind.

Feel your blood run through your veins
Trashing your brain like intercepting trains
Misfortune happened before you hurled
You were my gate to this world.

Names

They called me so many names
That day my life went up in flames
Don't raise more devils than you can lay down
Be sure to put them all in the ground.

I have no mercy, I have no grace
I have no regrets and I have no shame
I will play my wicked games
This is my evil and it has no name.

They called me so many names
That day my life went up in flames
They all thought that I was fake
Now they will all have a taste of my hate.

My list of names
My wicked games
My list of names
My wicked games.

Resurrected

Demons dancing on my grave
Thrilled by their victory
Now I've been sent away
From all my insanity.

What has become of me
The years of blood and pain
Rewarded me to be set free
I now live above the rain.

Resurrected into another being
My soul has gained a new meaning
Now I live to silently sing
I've got a message to bring.

Keep your eyes closed

I see dead bodies everywhere
I walk where you talk
I scream where you stay silent.

But my scream is a far away cry
In a misty wind where the angels sin
Where they have forgotten who they are.

In this place even the angels looks to the sky
For answers, for peace.
This place I talk off You know well.

Haven't you noticed? Have you been sleeping?
This is where we kill each other Over money and fame
This is where we embrace the pain
And trust me this place does not need devils
As we do not know shame.

This is a place where we love each other
in order to feel better about ourselves.

NO!! No more...
You have created a monster out of me
That's why you should close your eyes
And keep them closed
Only to hear a demon whisper in the wind
Let me, Let me, Let me in.

My War

I got a knife of sadness in my heart
I am empty as I rip love apart
With a broken body and soul
I lose all sense of control.

This is my war

As you once threw me to the ground
Now it's time to take back what's truly mine
I got scars from head to toe
From a battle a long time ago.

This is my war

Drag me through hell for my past mistakes
My hatred for you again awakes
The truth to finally be revealed
In the dreaded mist at the battlefield.

Malvy

Let the sin begin
You I welcome in
I know it's what you seek
But what I don't need I'll keep.

You need what I got
But I deny you until you rot
The pleasure of saying no
And turn my back and go.

Deliver me

Feed me with courage to step out of line
These memories has forced me, into hatred, into crime
My head is full of questions, that I just can't leave behind
And selfishness has blinded me again.. now.

Climb down from your chair, there's no escape my dear
I can't love you, I can't love you
Now this is my last song.

Feed me with courage to speak freely now
Pierce our souls together, I only love you when you cry
Burry all these dreams, forget about how it feels
I've waited for this moment all my life.

So kill your last memorie, that you have of me
I will never be the same again.

I'm so full of hate, releasing it feels so great
Now deliver me, deliver me to my fate.

ANAGRAMS

MY EDGY ART
My tragedy

A METAL HUG
Laugh at me

DARK INSERT
Drink tears

NOW CAPTURED
A new product

MY LORD WEPT
Empty world

COPYING BRIDE
Body piercing

EGOMANIAC COWARDS
Come cowards again

RUDEST PENIS
US President

GROIN LIE
Religion

BC RICH GUITARS
A bright circus

LIVE
Evil

RAT
Art

RESIST
Sister

FUNERAL
Real fun

THE EYES
They see

About the Author

Adrian Guldahl is a poet and a recording artist,
This is his first collection of printed poetry.

This is the reissued version of the original from 2009
With added poems and lyrics.

FSC
www.fsc.org
MIX
Papir fra
bærekraftige kilder
Paper from
responsible sources
FSC® C105338